Simple Gifts

Shaker Tune
Arr. M.Verhaalen

Flowing

mf

5

8

f

12

f

15

mf

rit.

pp

Old Joe Clark

American Folk Song
Marion Verhaalen

Song of the Night

Marion Verhaalen

Minka

Marion Verhaalen
Slavic Folk Song

Briskly

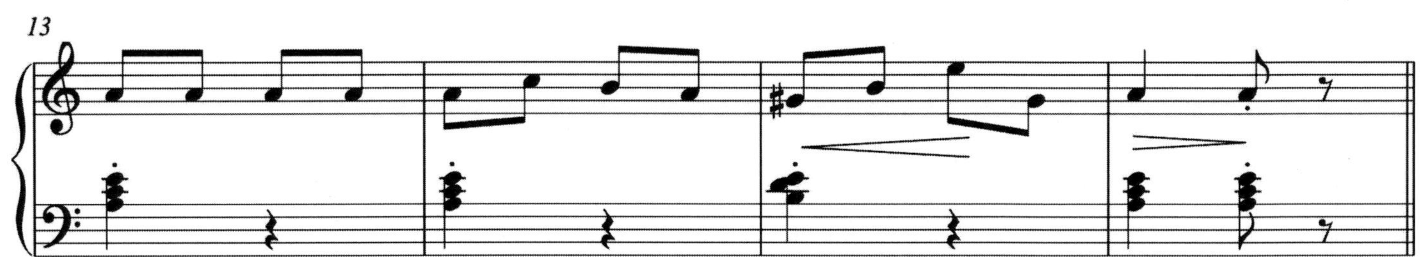

VARIATION

17 Smooth as Ice

Chaconne

Marion Verhaalen

Smoothly

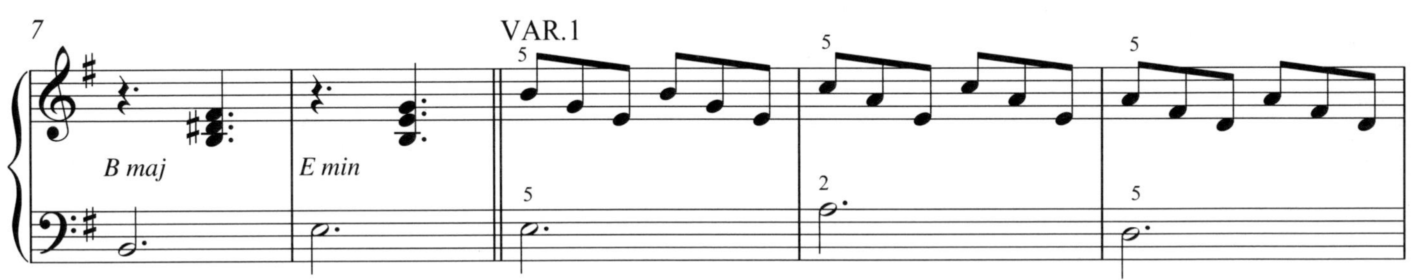

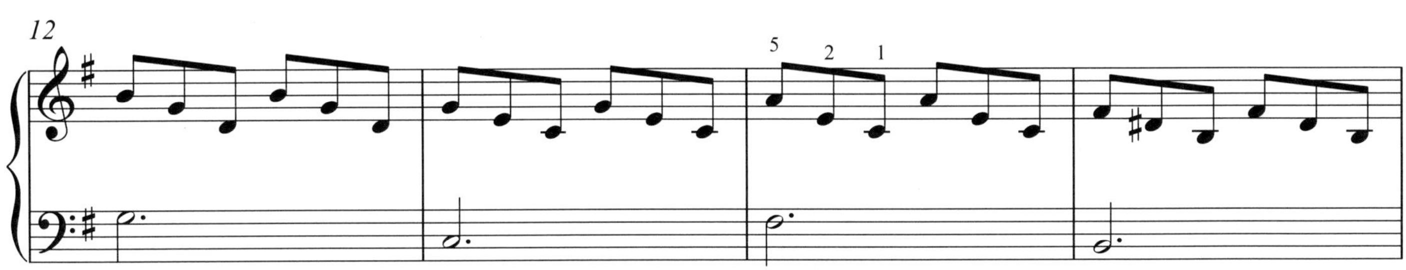

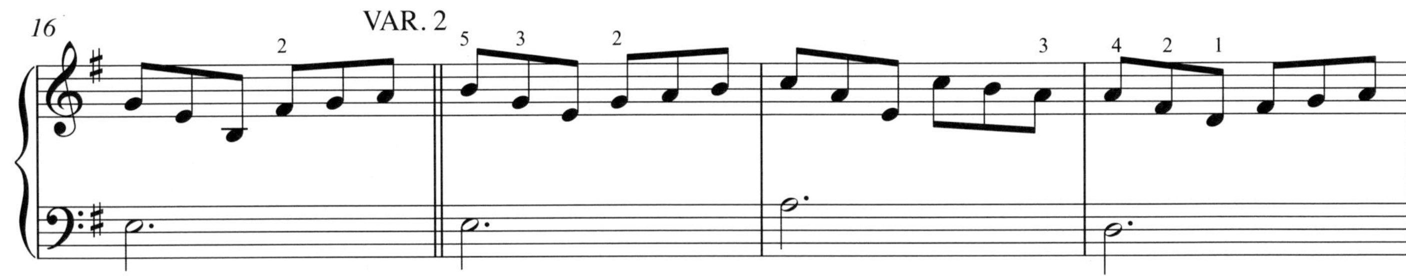

VAR. 3
27
30
VAR. 4
34
38
Continue making
your own variations.

Renaissance Melody

Italian Song
Adapted/Arr. M. Verhaalen

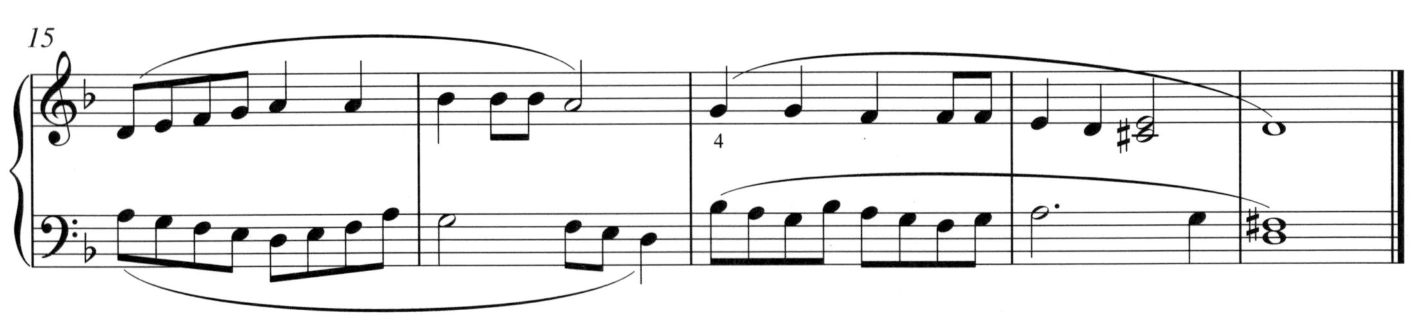